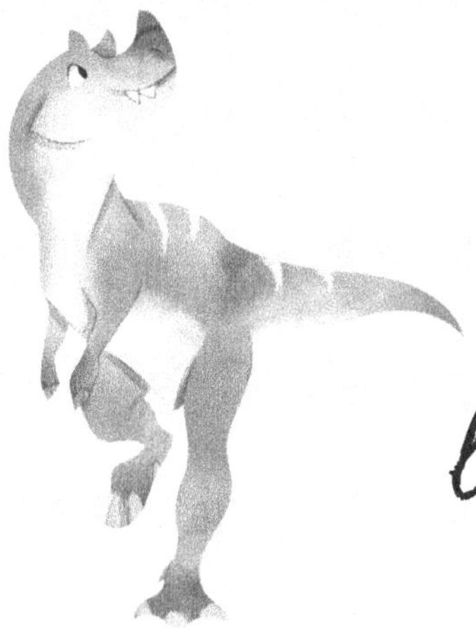

this book belongs to:

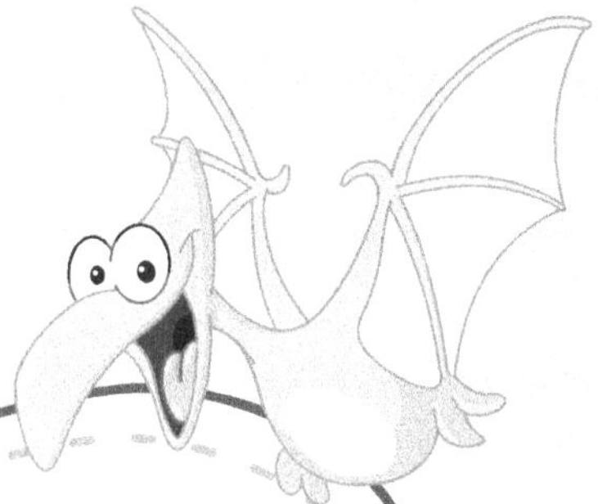

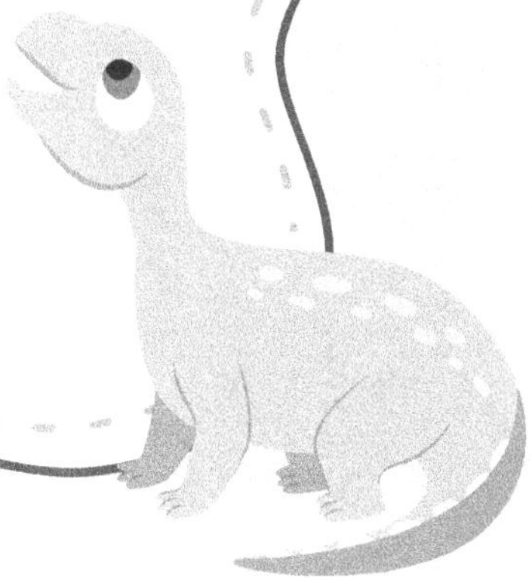

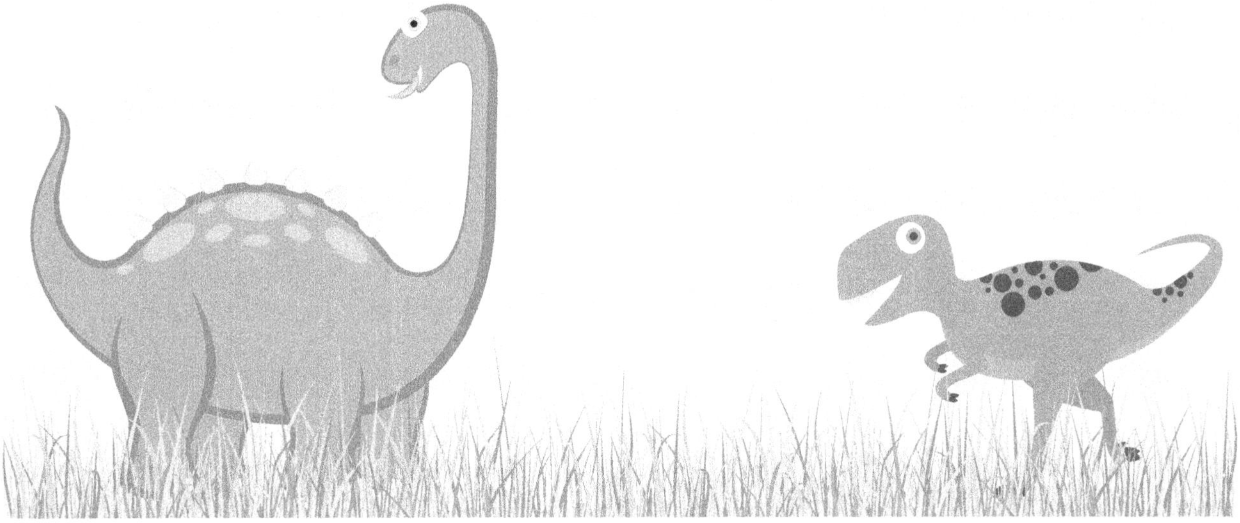

We wish you the best time coloring this book. Don't forget to write all the letters. For even more fun, you can sing the alphabet song.

Study shuttle

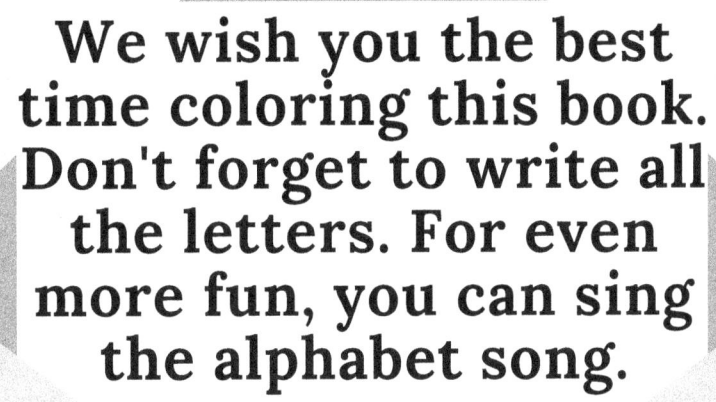

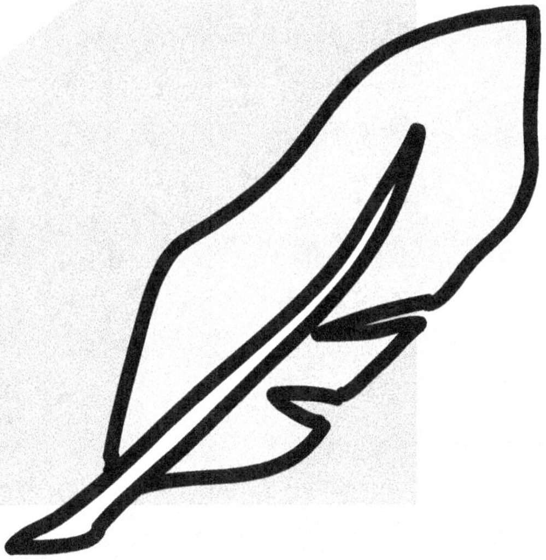

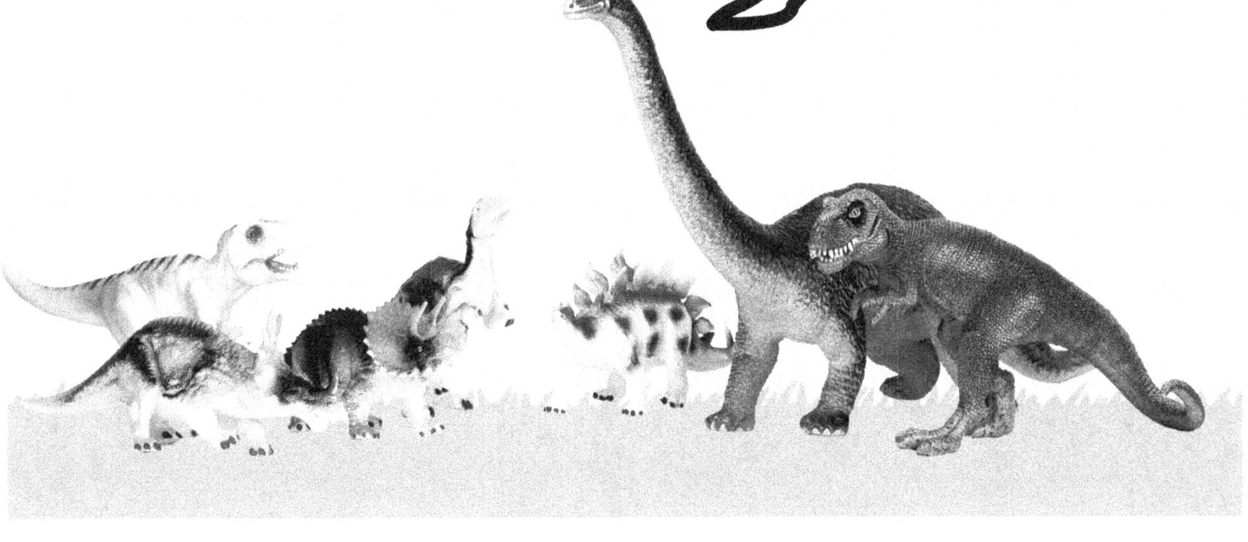

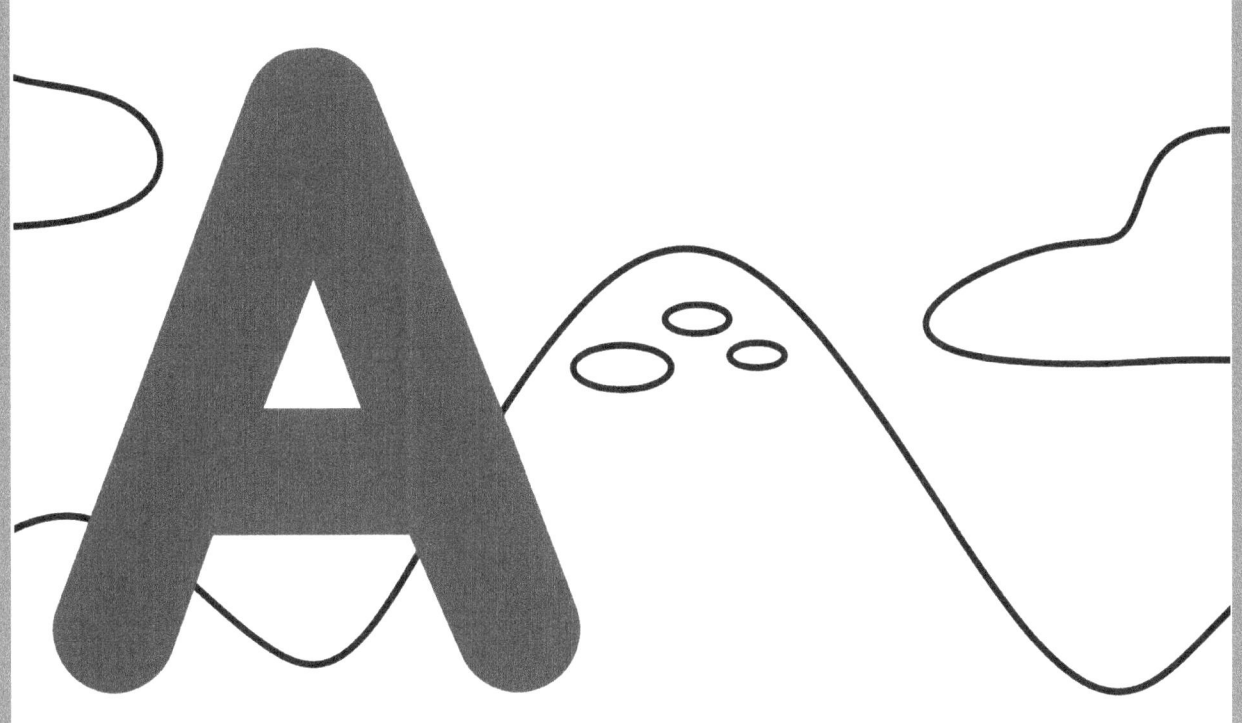

Ankylosaurus

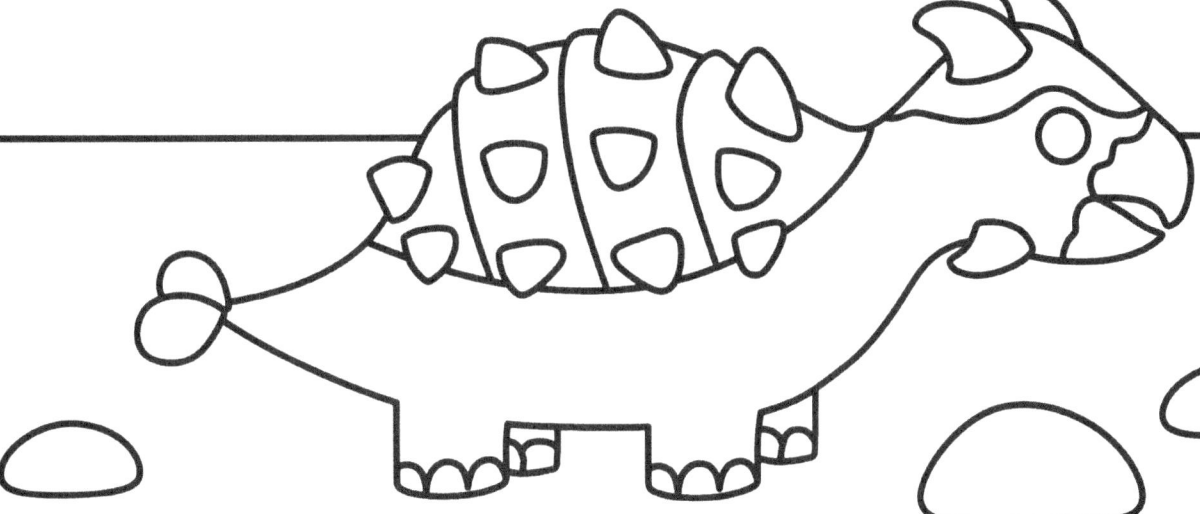

Write the letter:

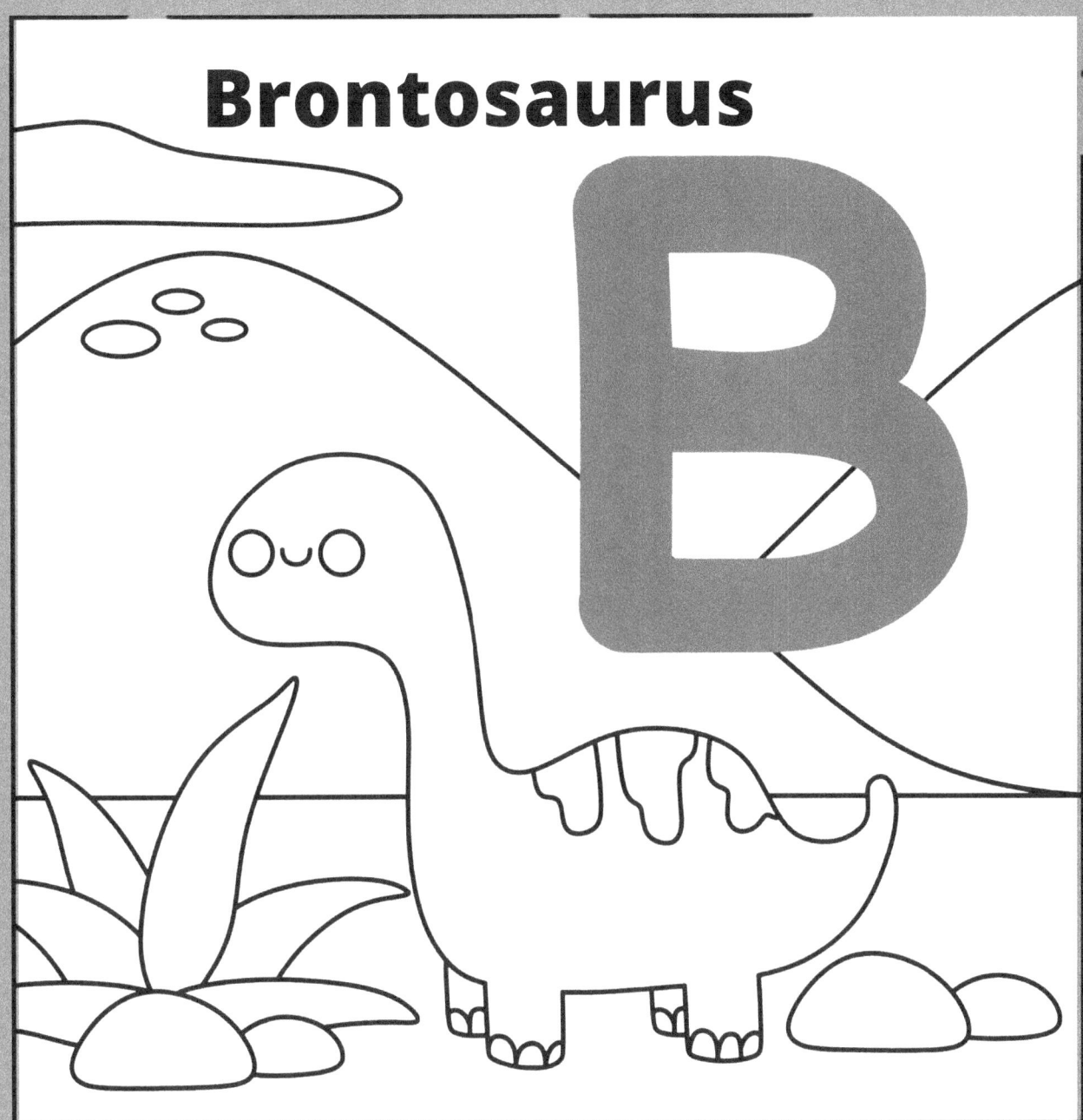

Write the letter:

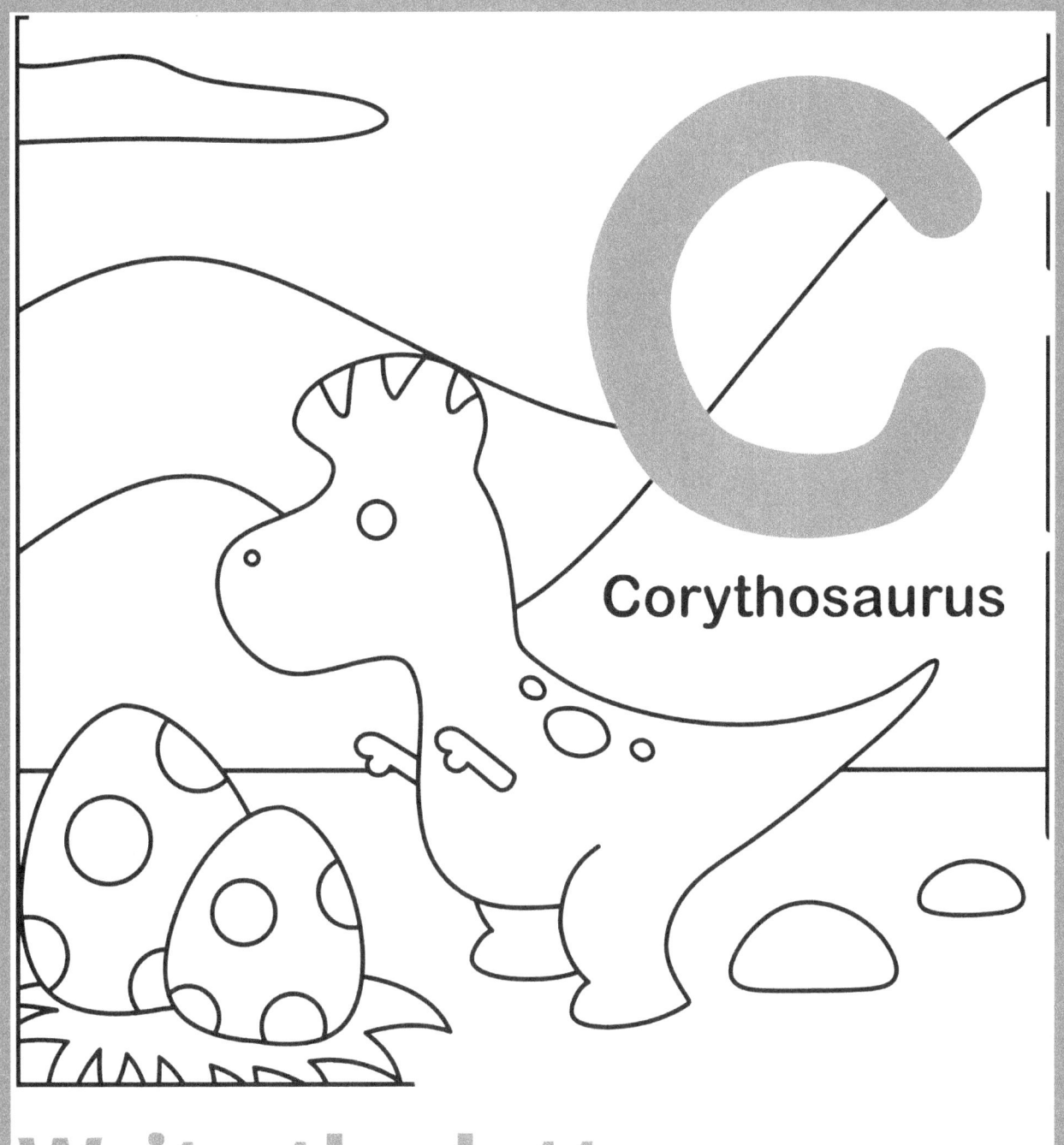

Corythosaurus

Write the letter:

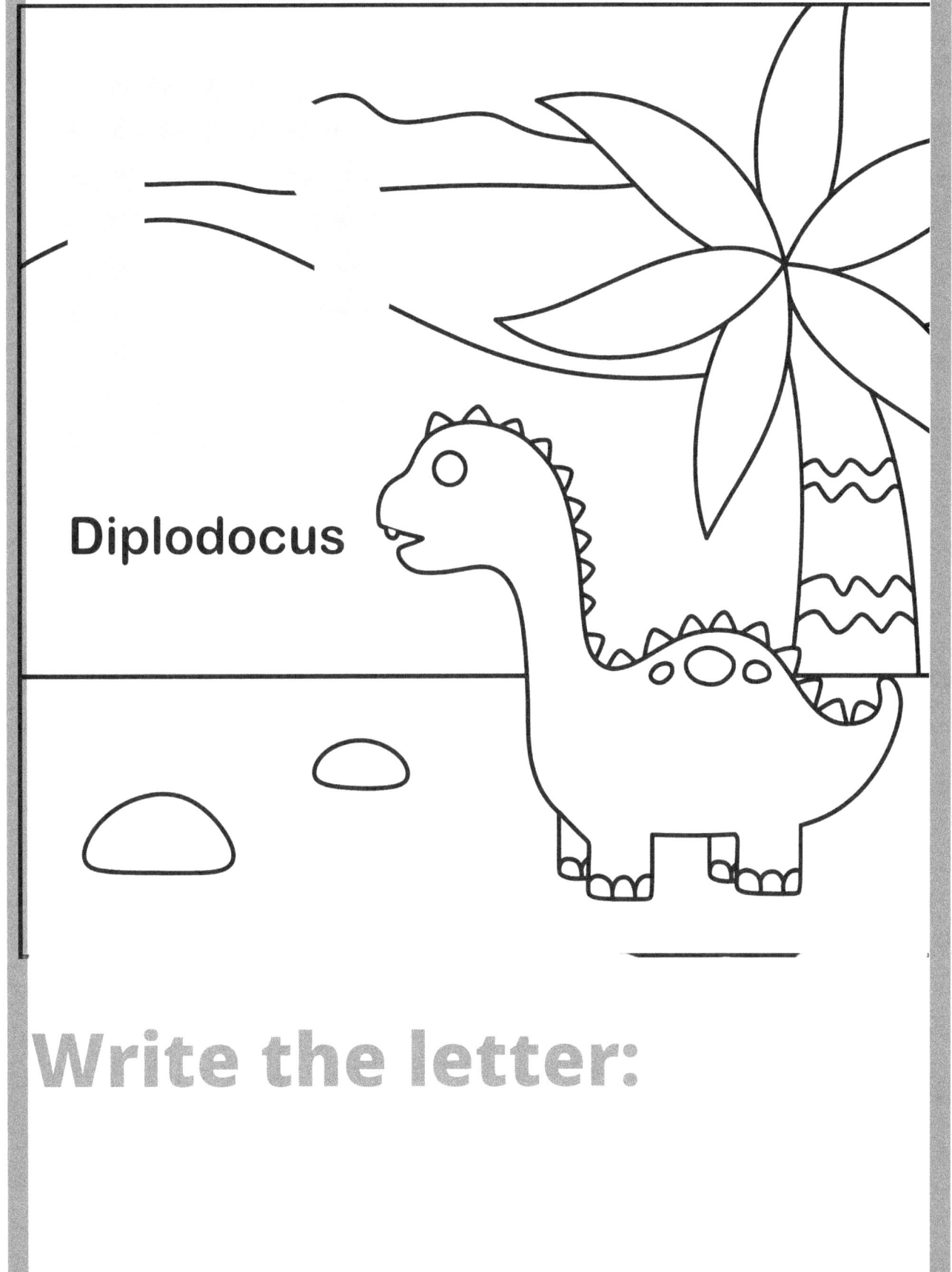

Diplodocus

Write the letter:

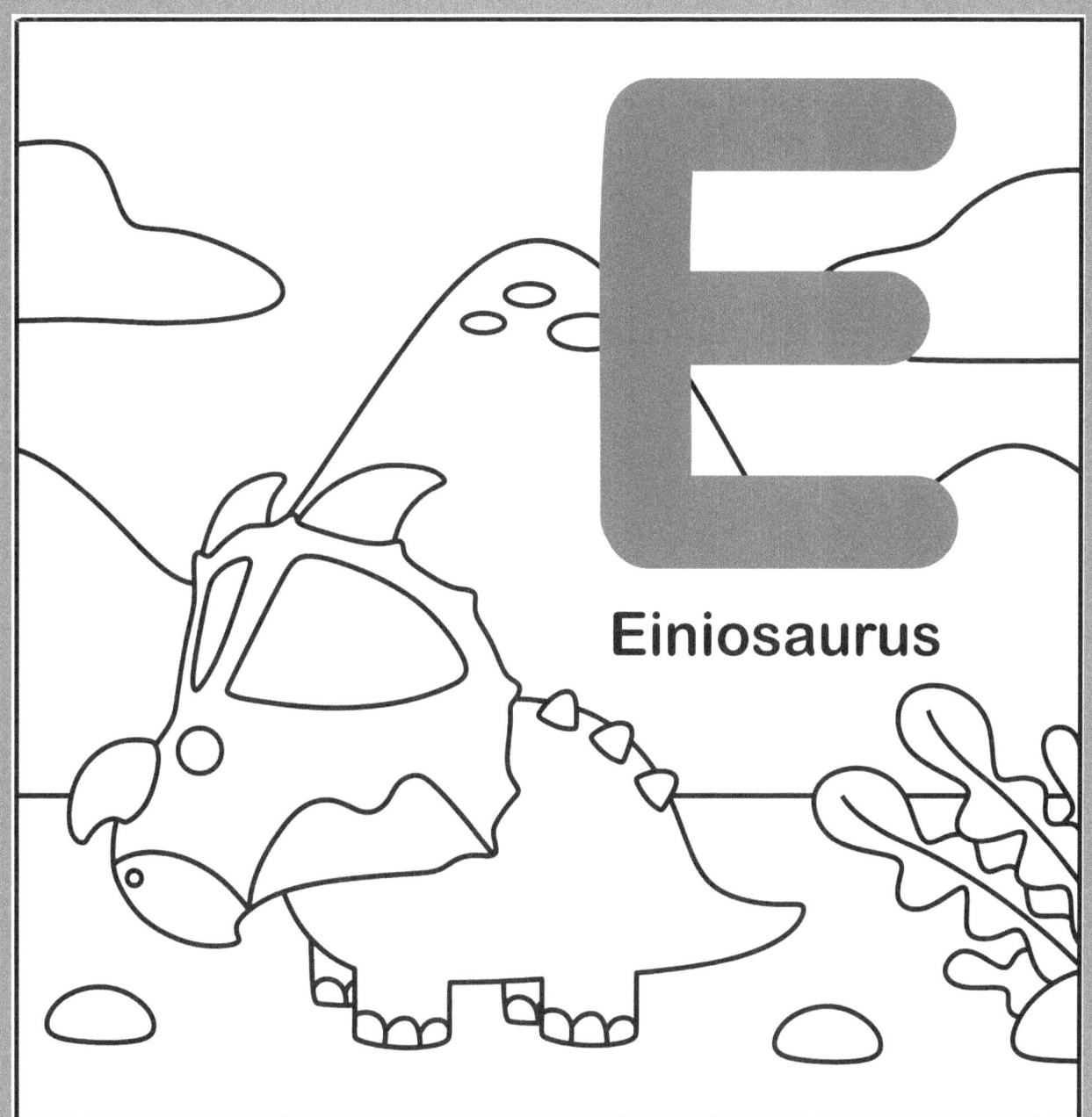

Einiosaurus

Write the letter:

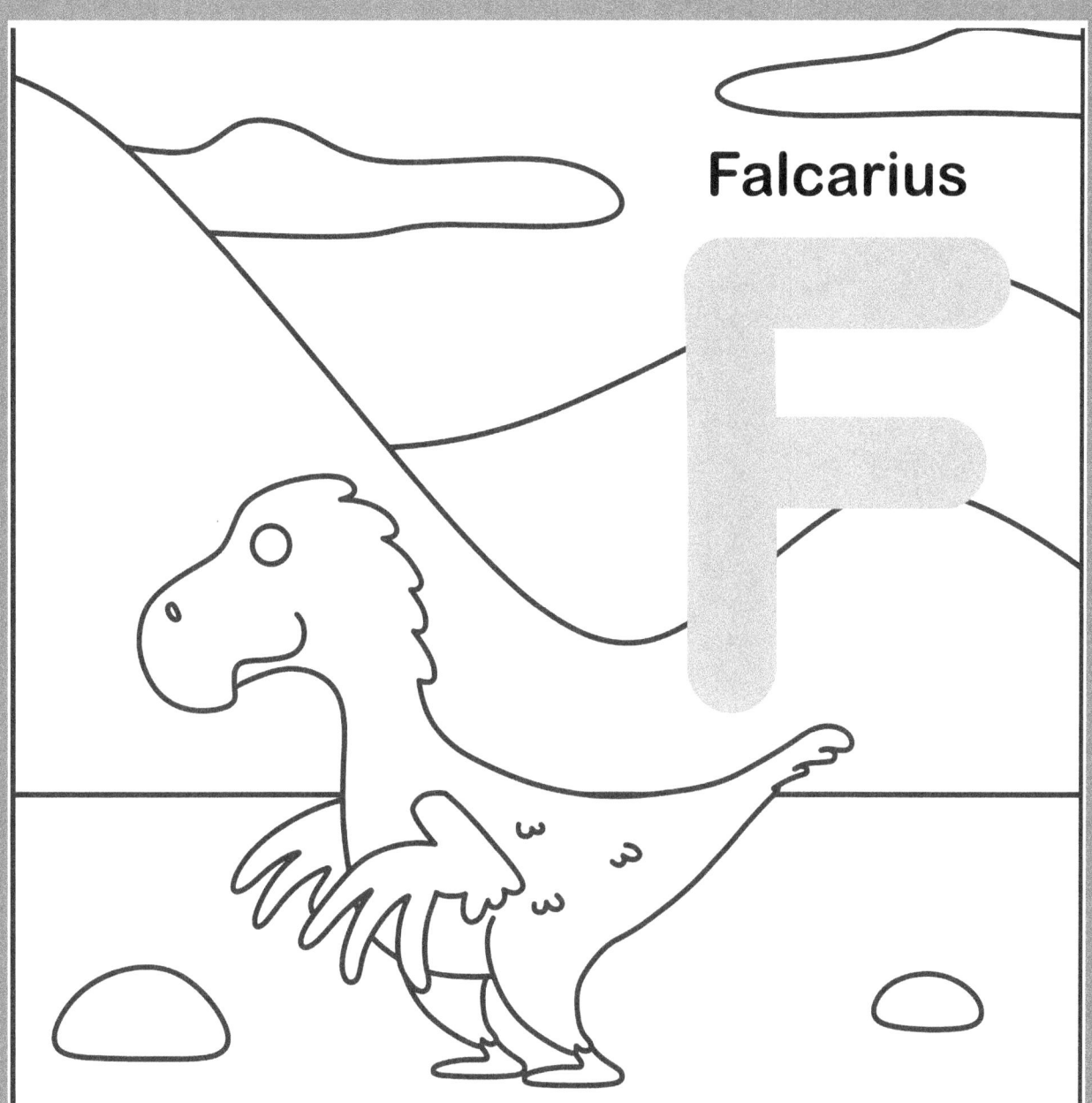

Gallimimus

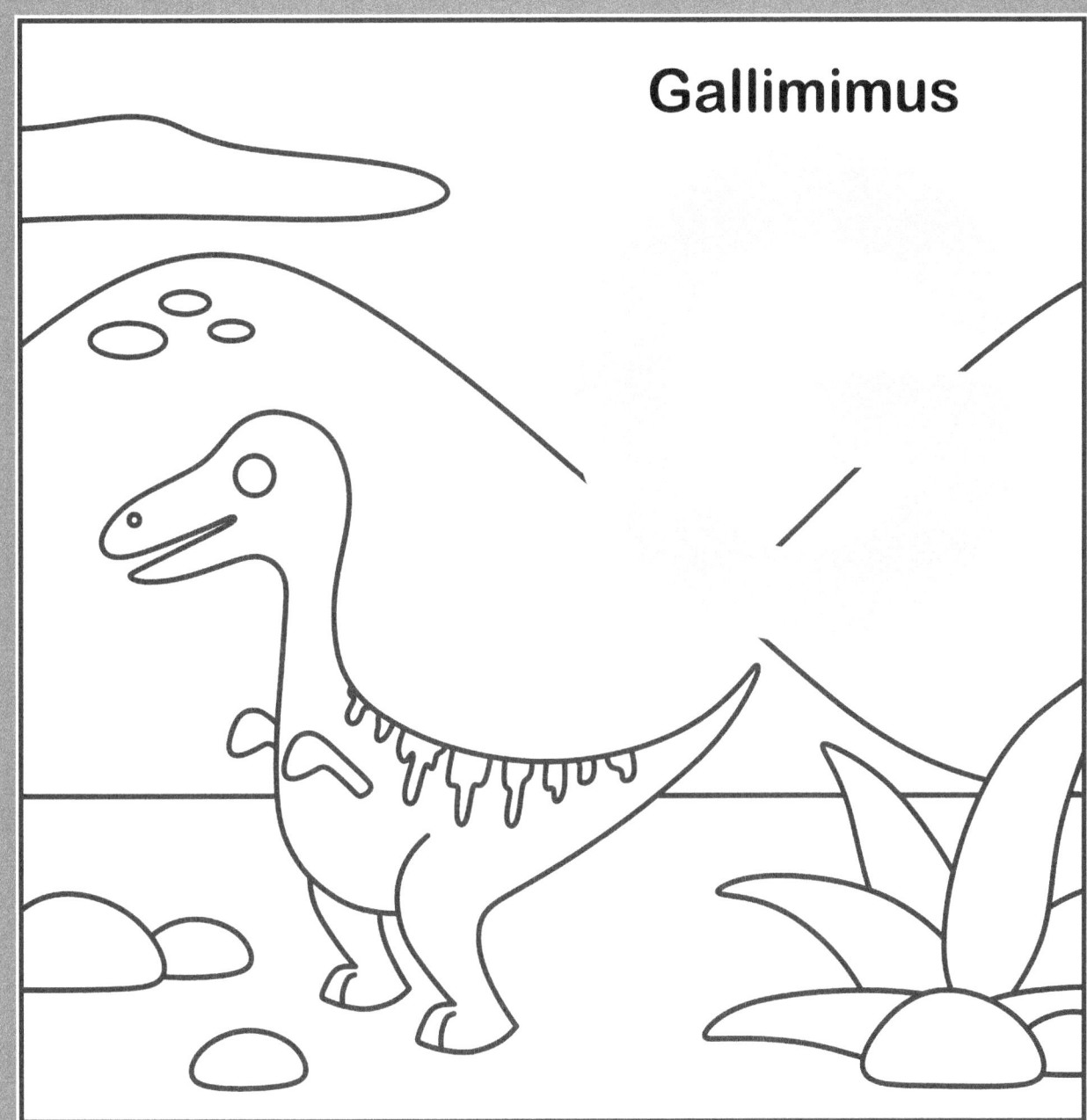

Write the letter:

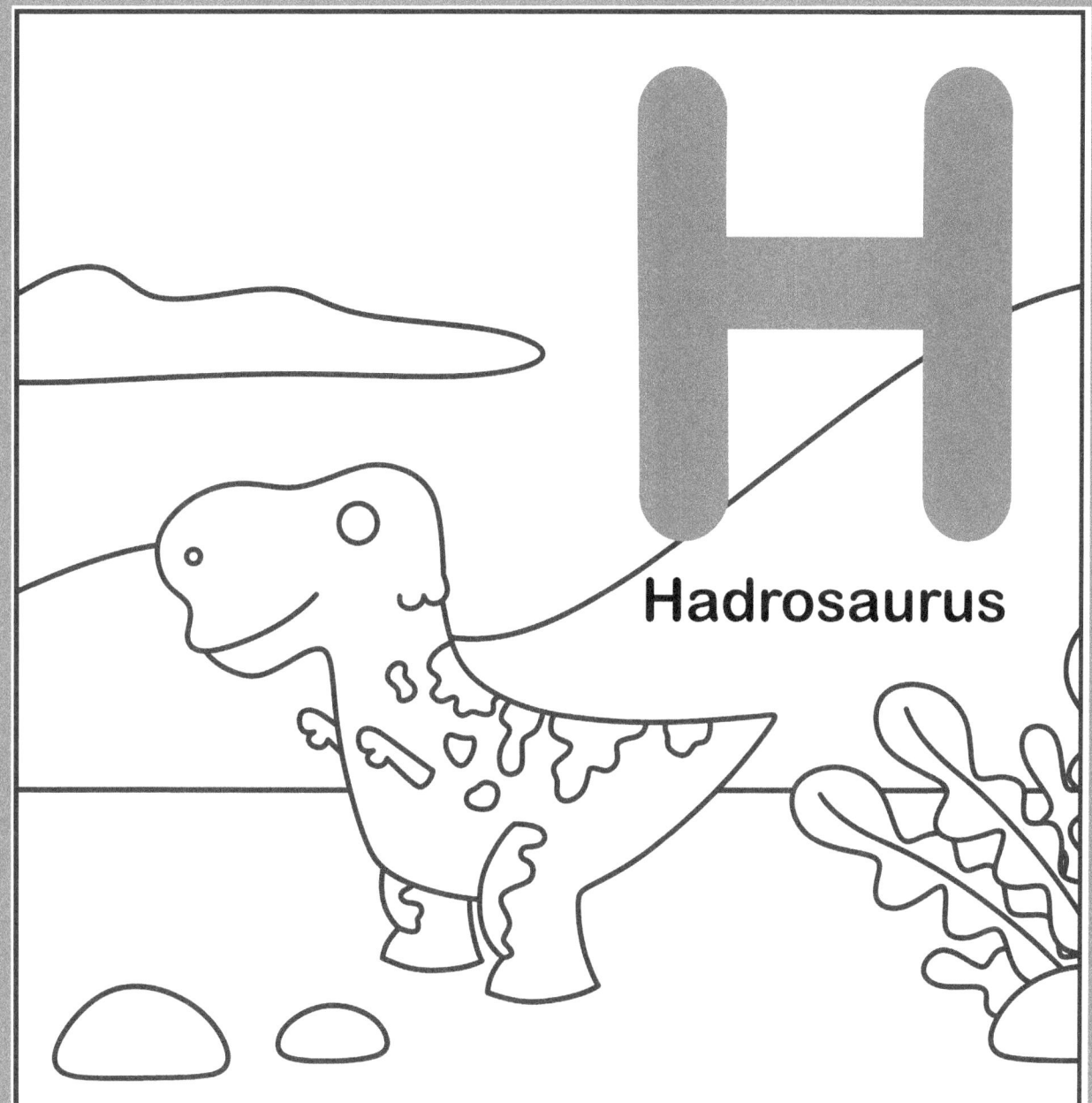

Hadrosaurus

Write the letter:

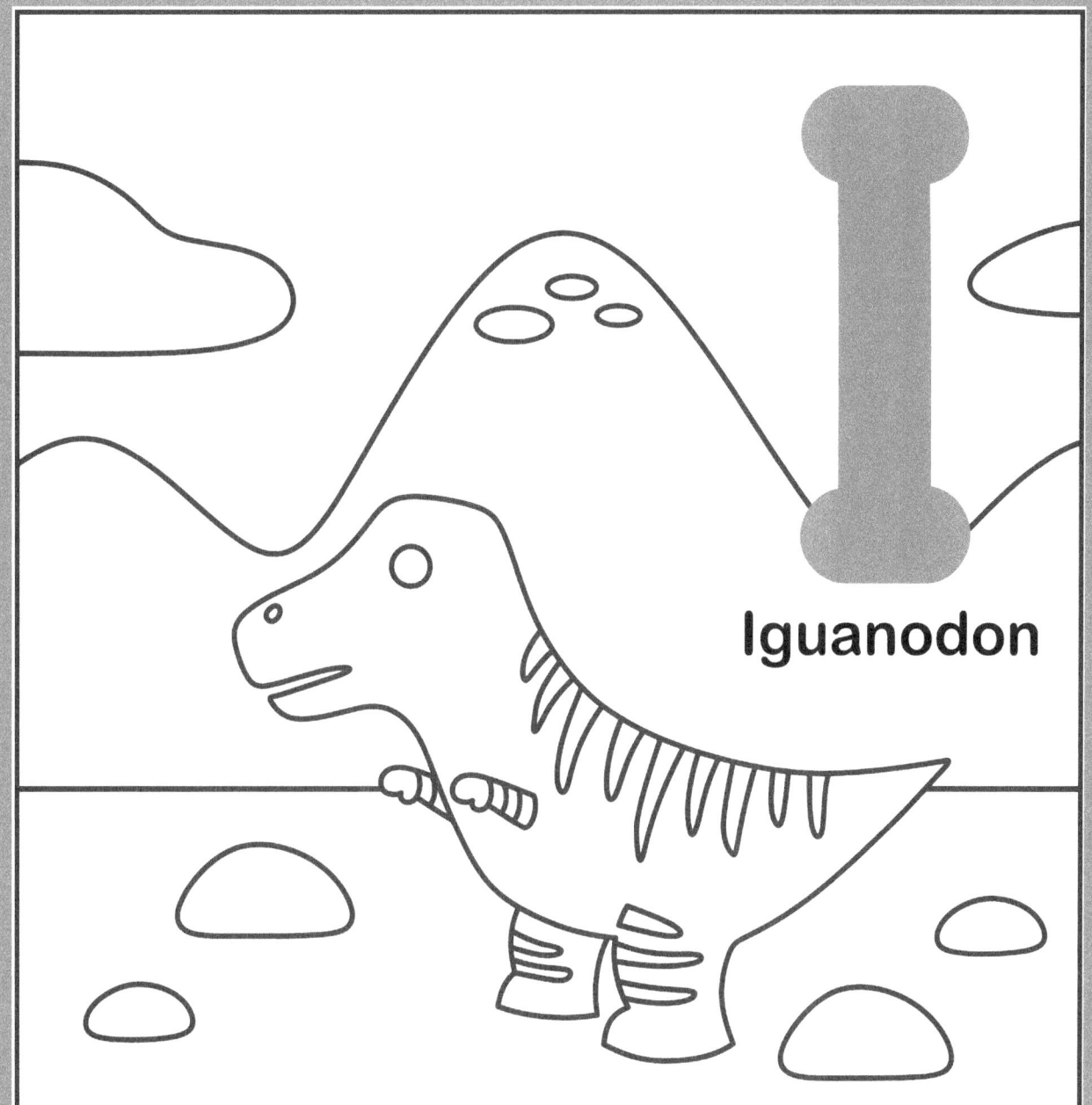

Iguanodon

Write the letter:

Jaxartosaurus

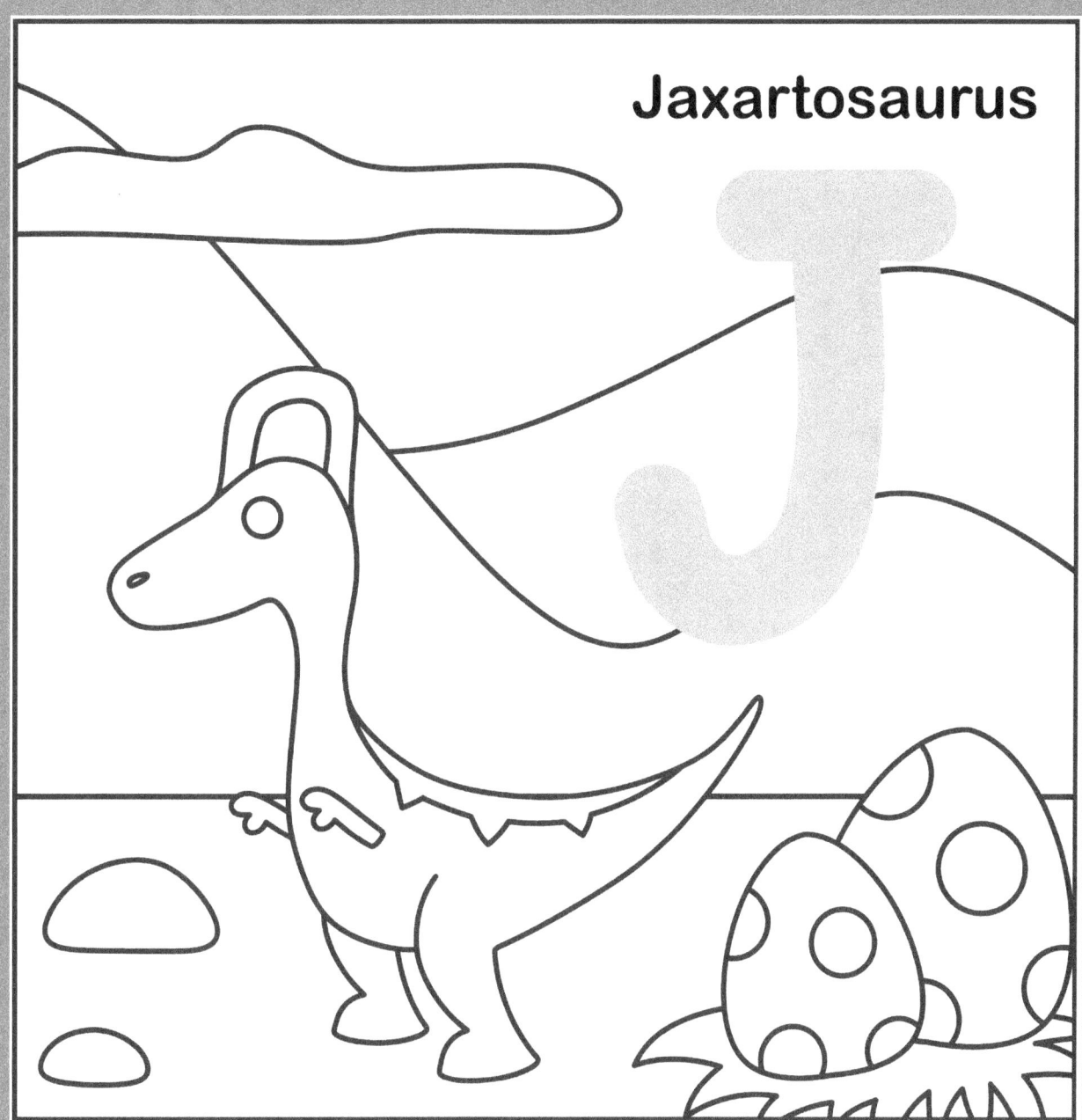

Write the letter:

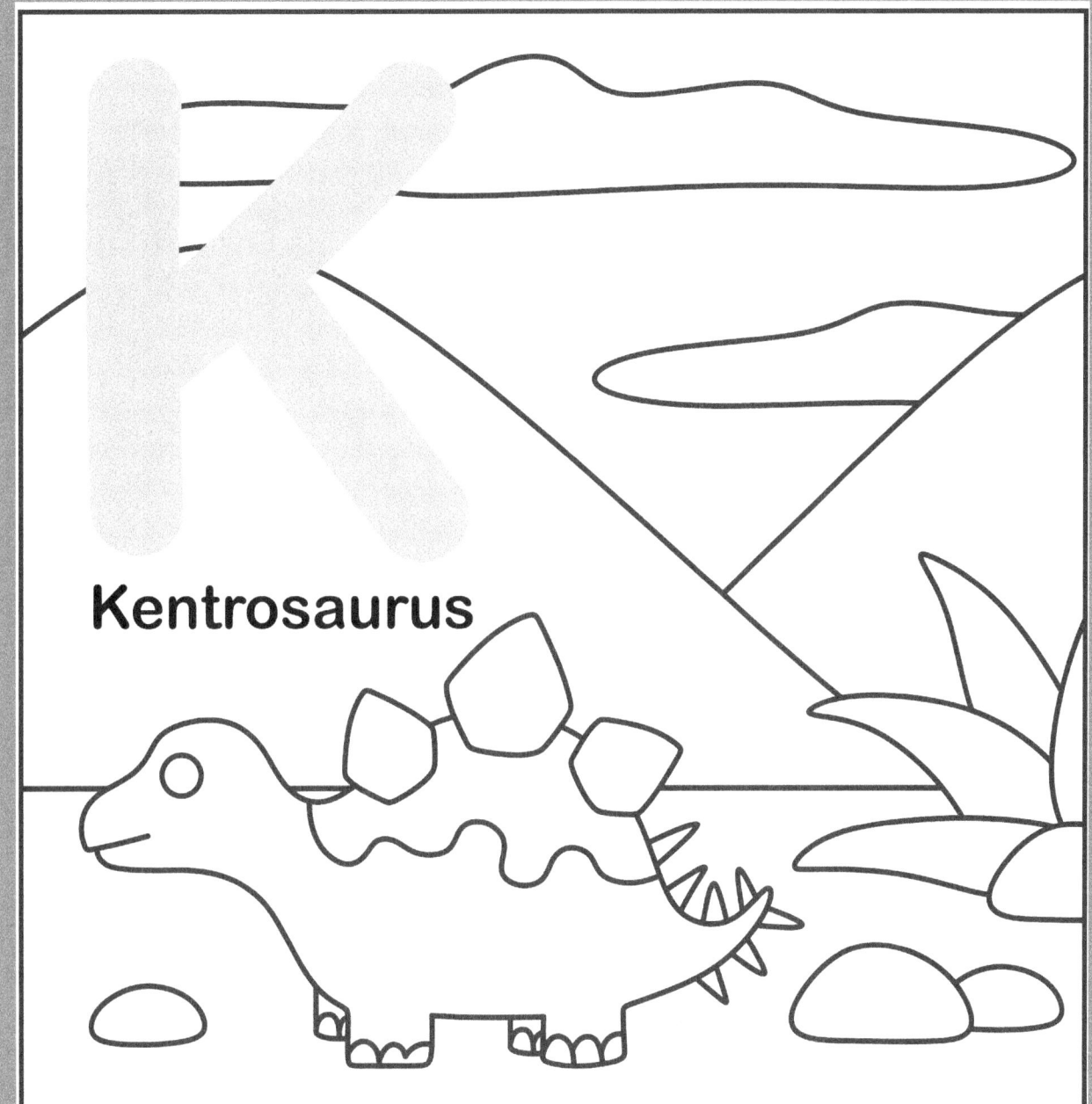

Kentrosaurus

Write the letter:

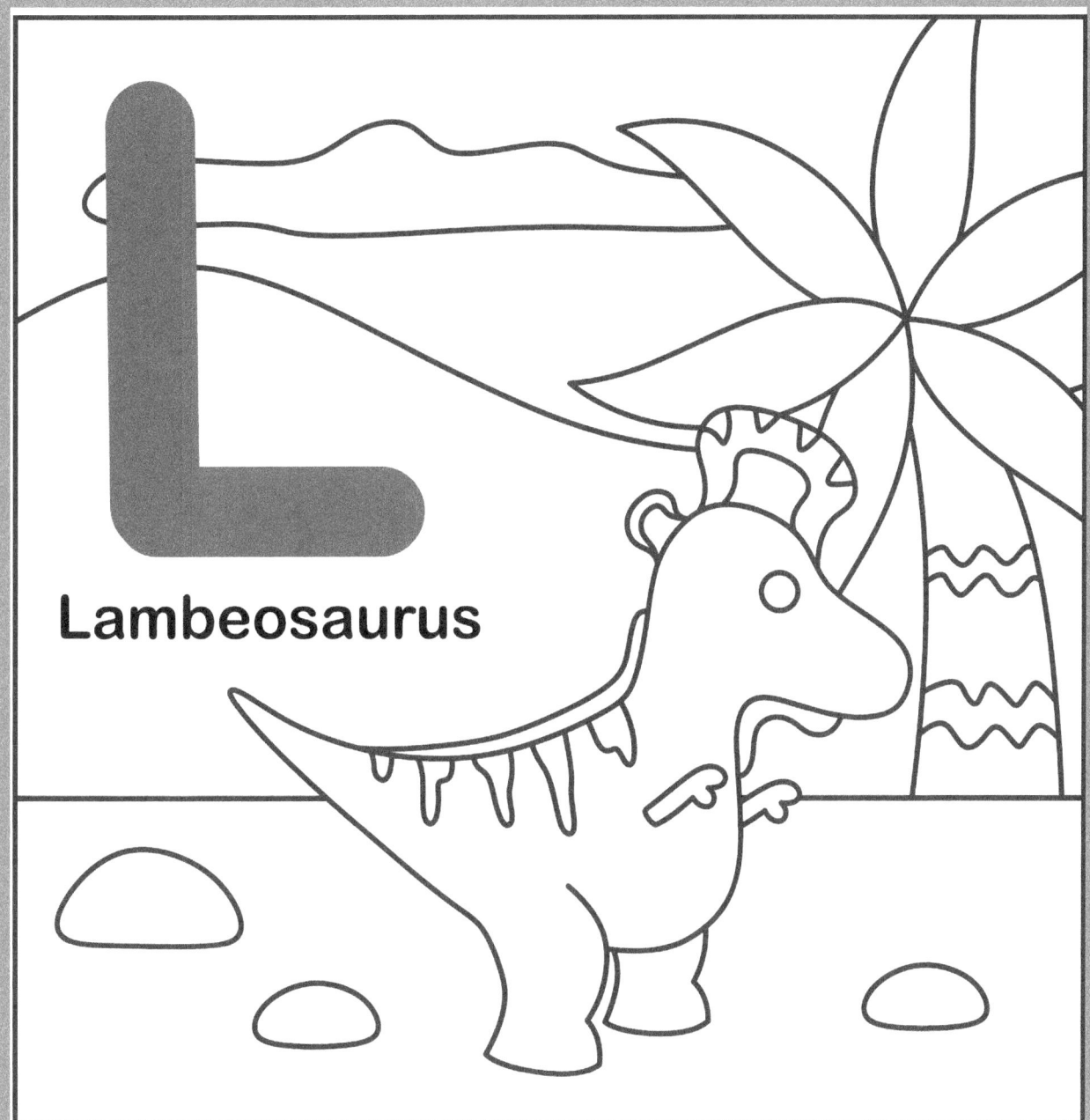

Lambeosaurus

Write the letter:

Monolophosaurus

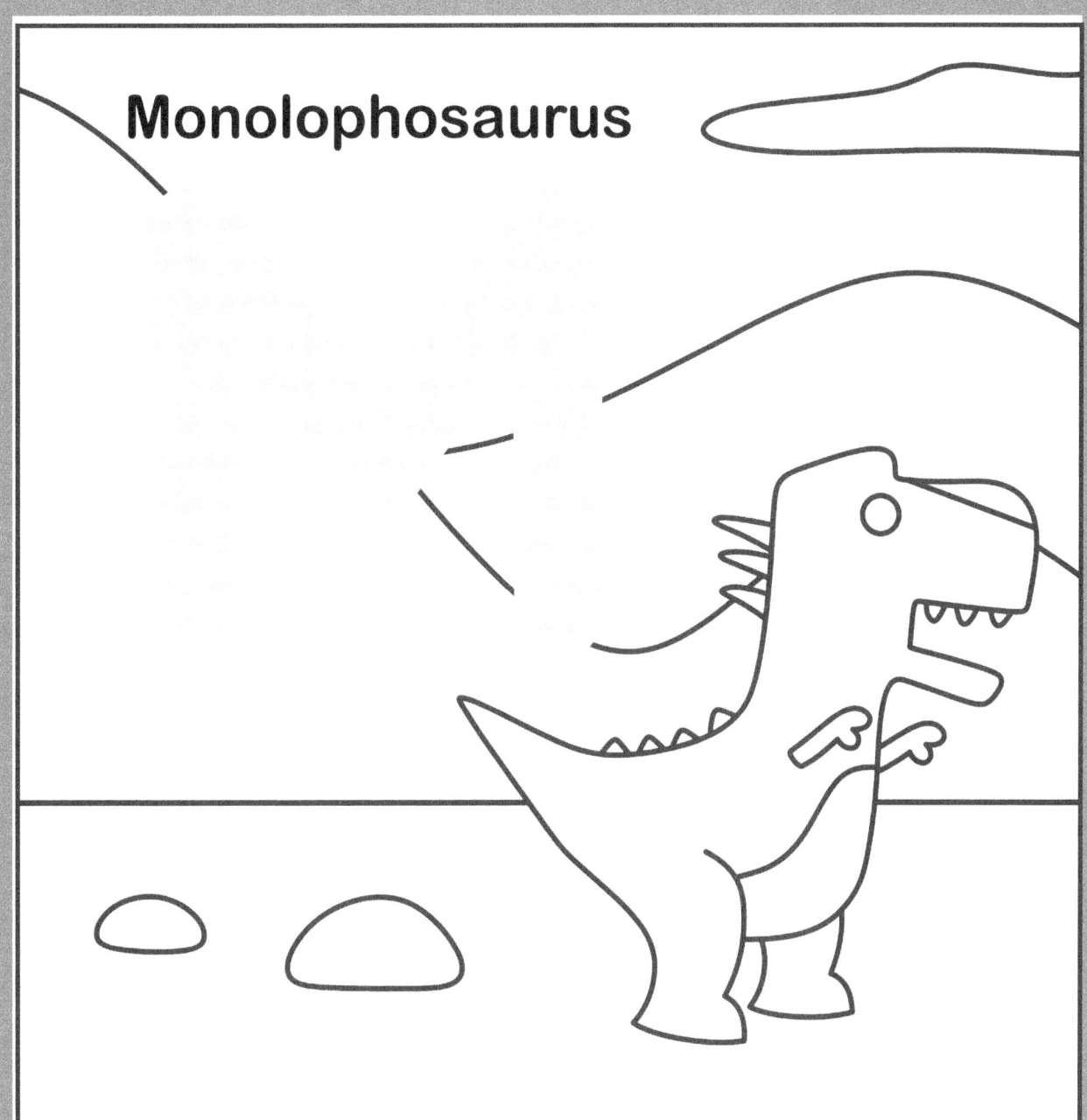

Write the letter:

Nomingia

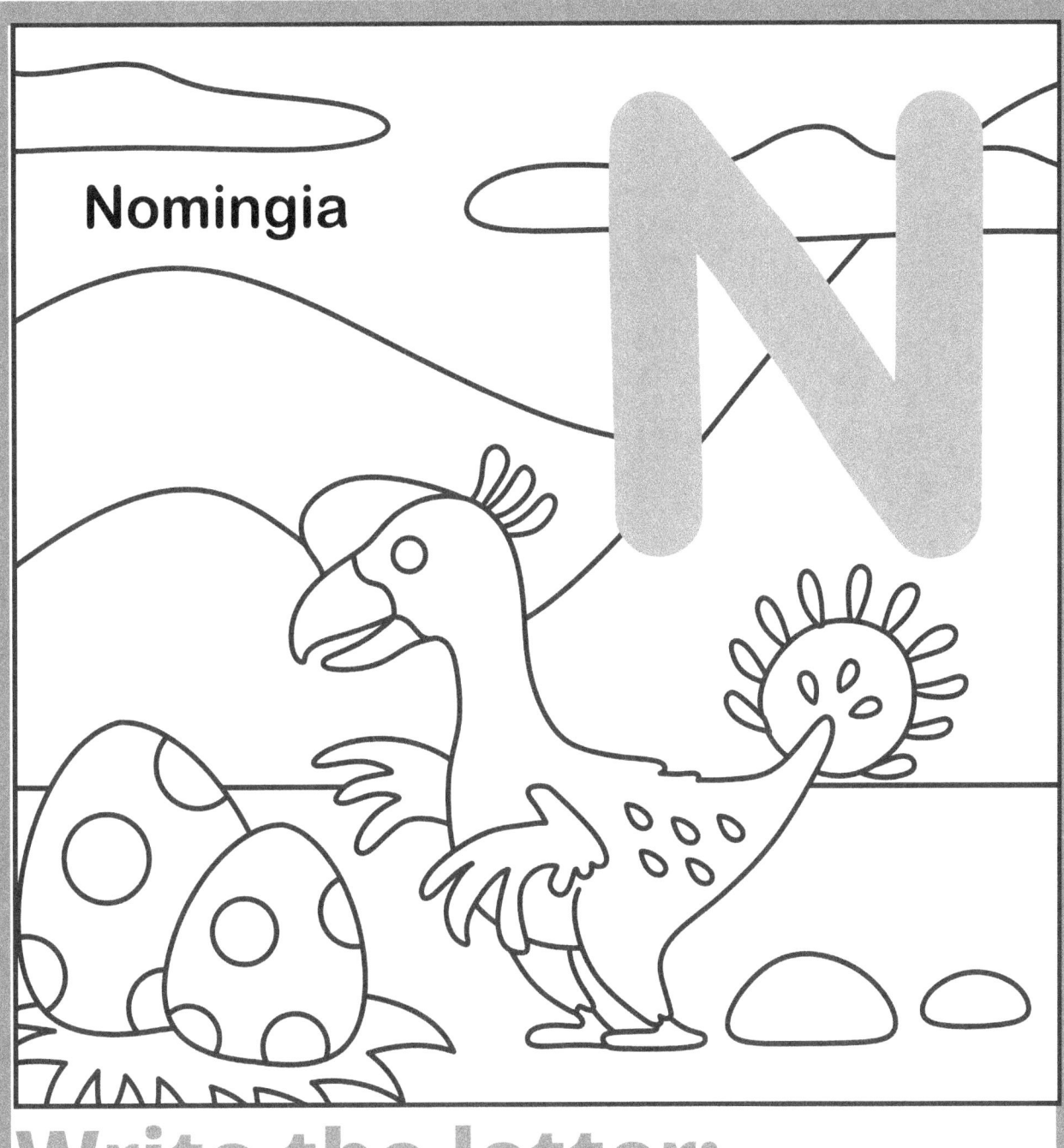

Write the letter:

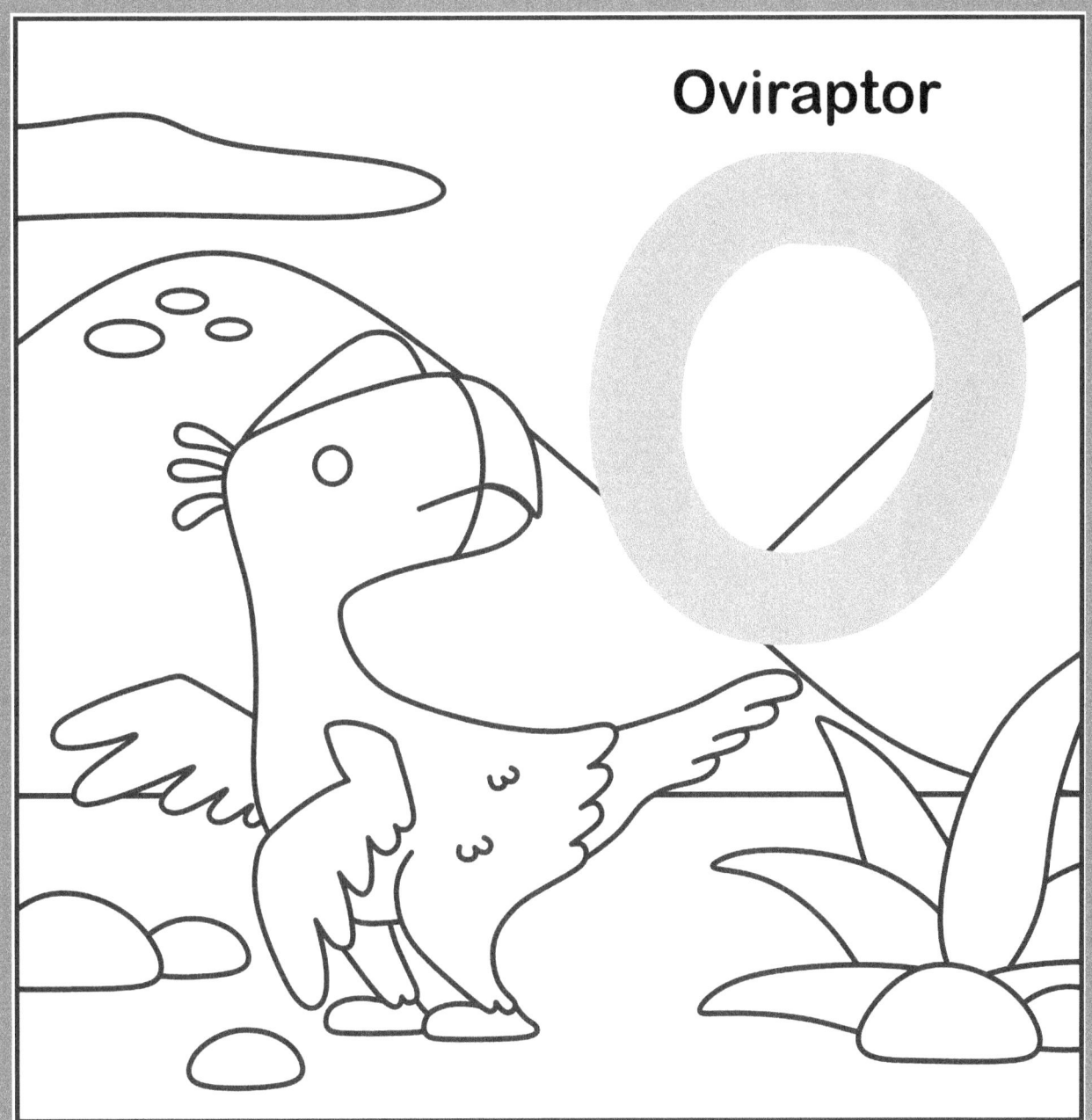

Oviraptor

Write the letter:

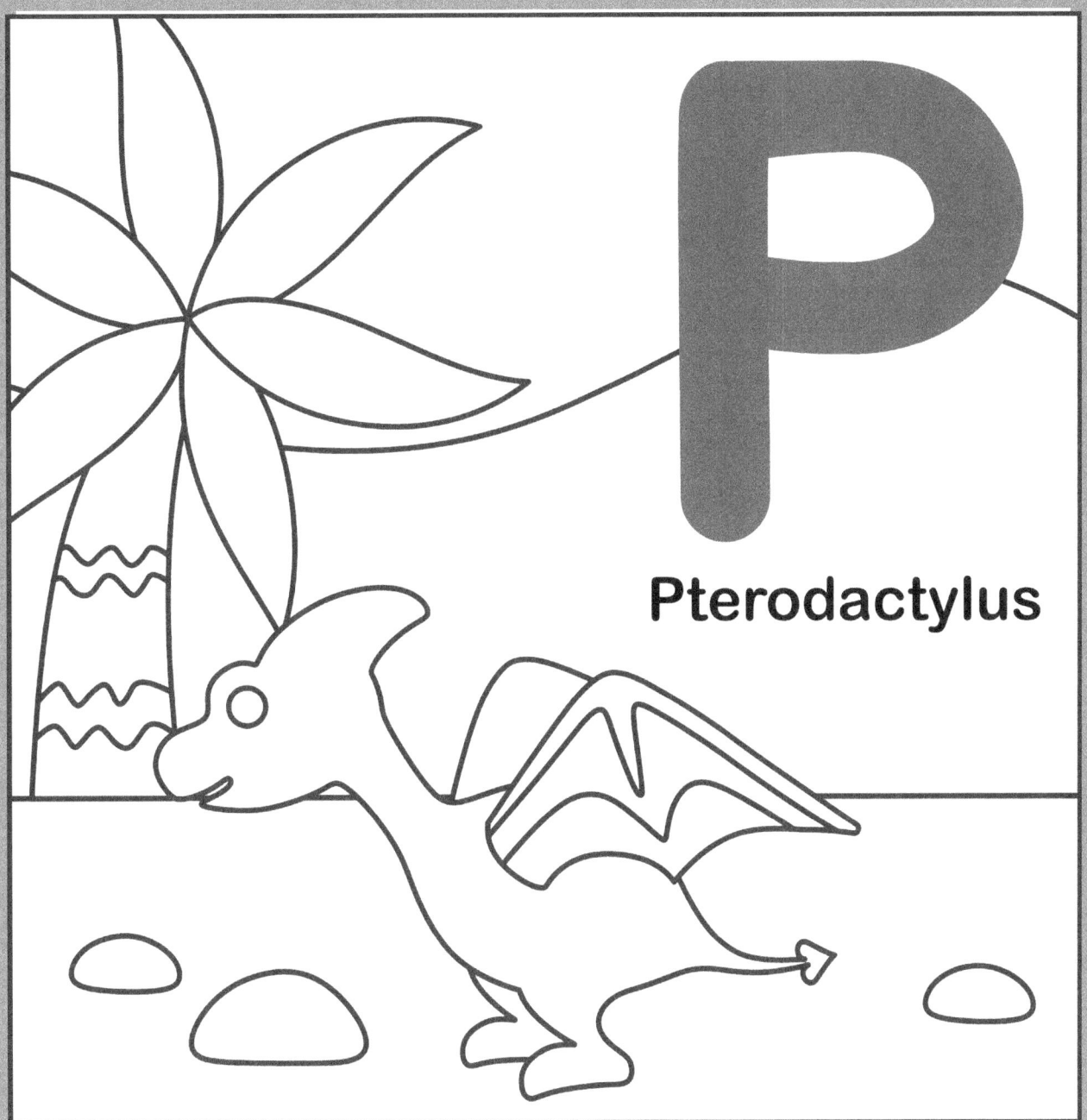

Pterodactylus

Write the letter:

Quetzalcoatlus

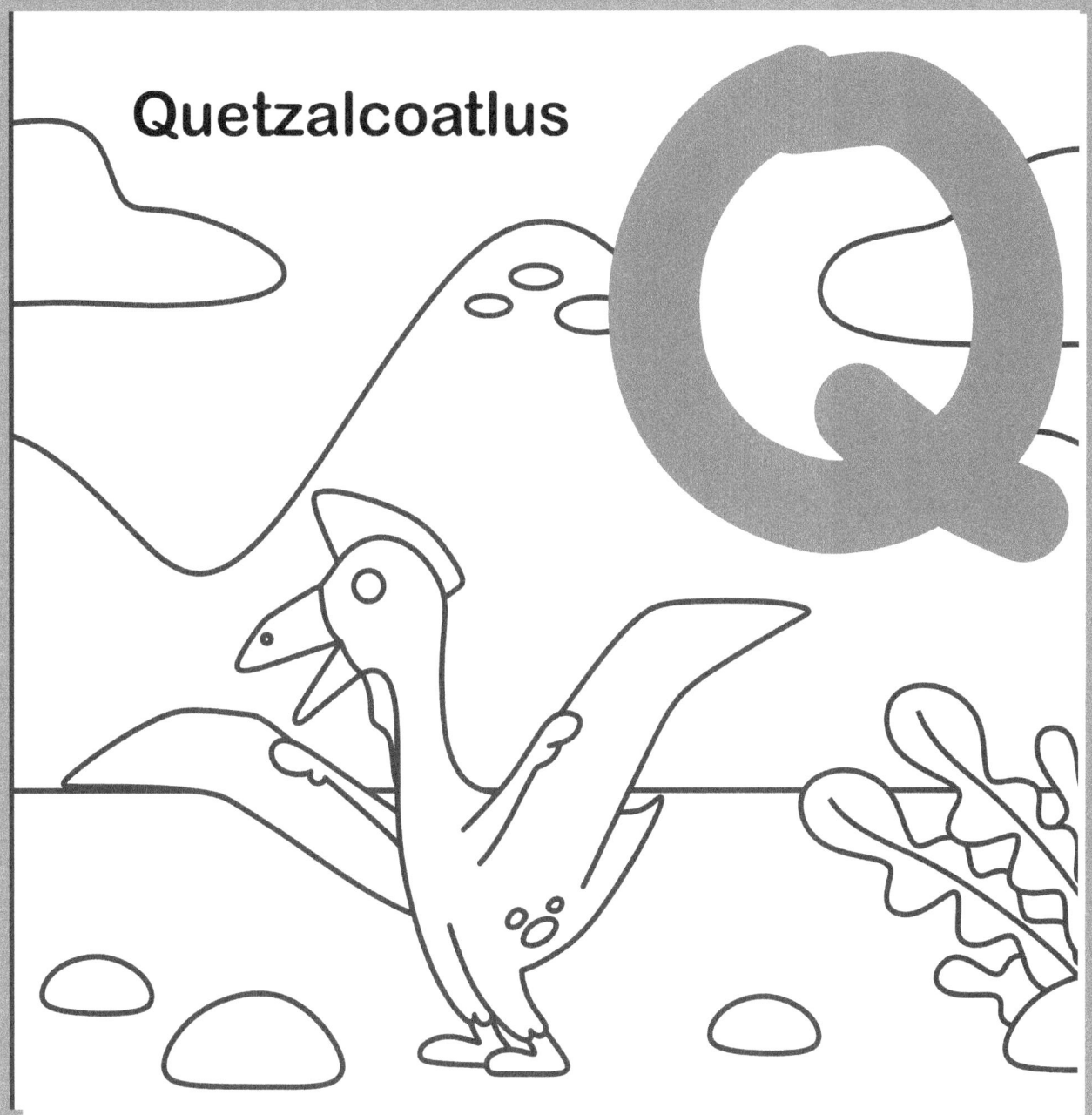

Write the letter:

Regaliceratops

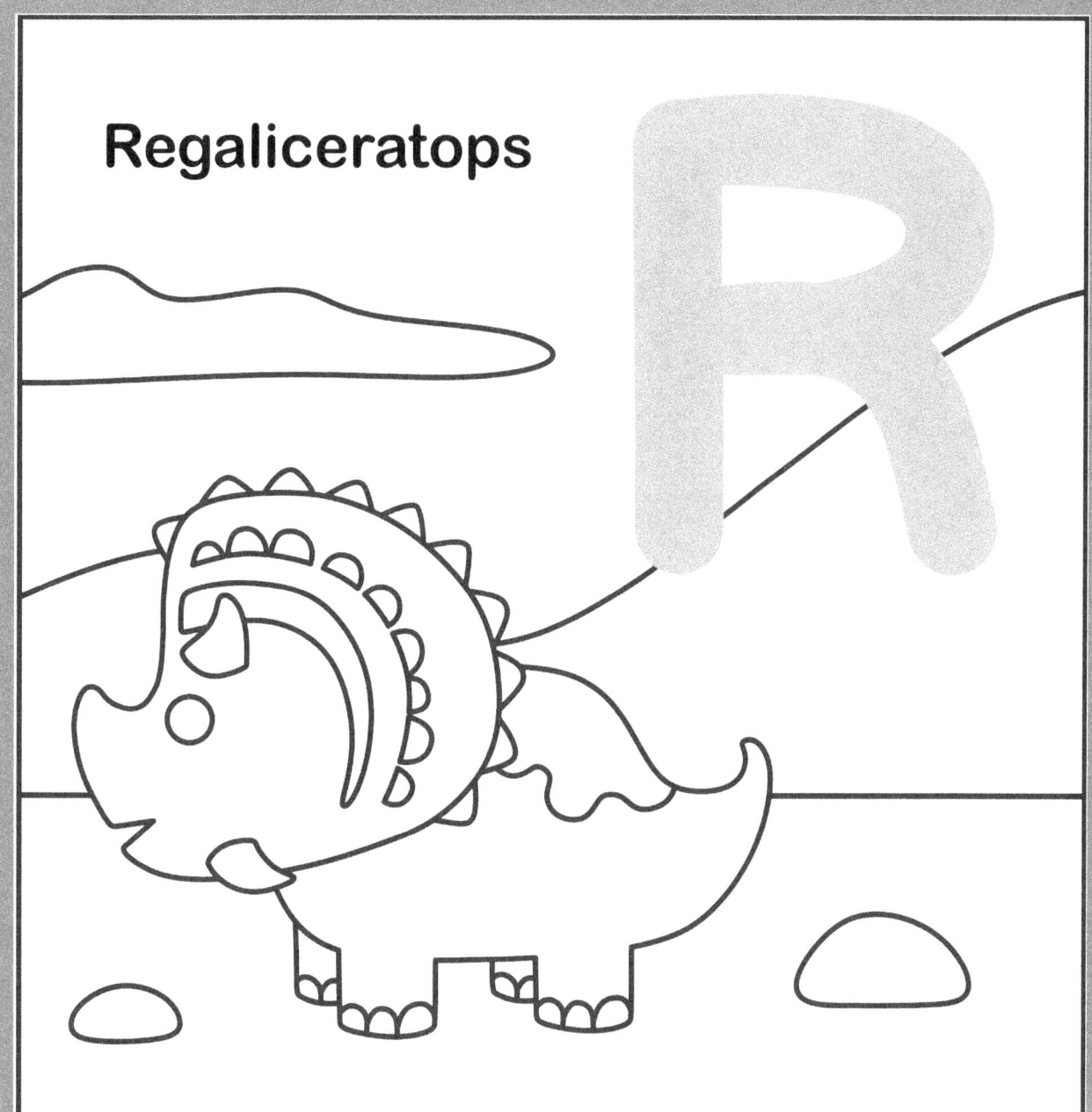

Write the letter:

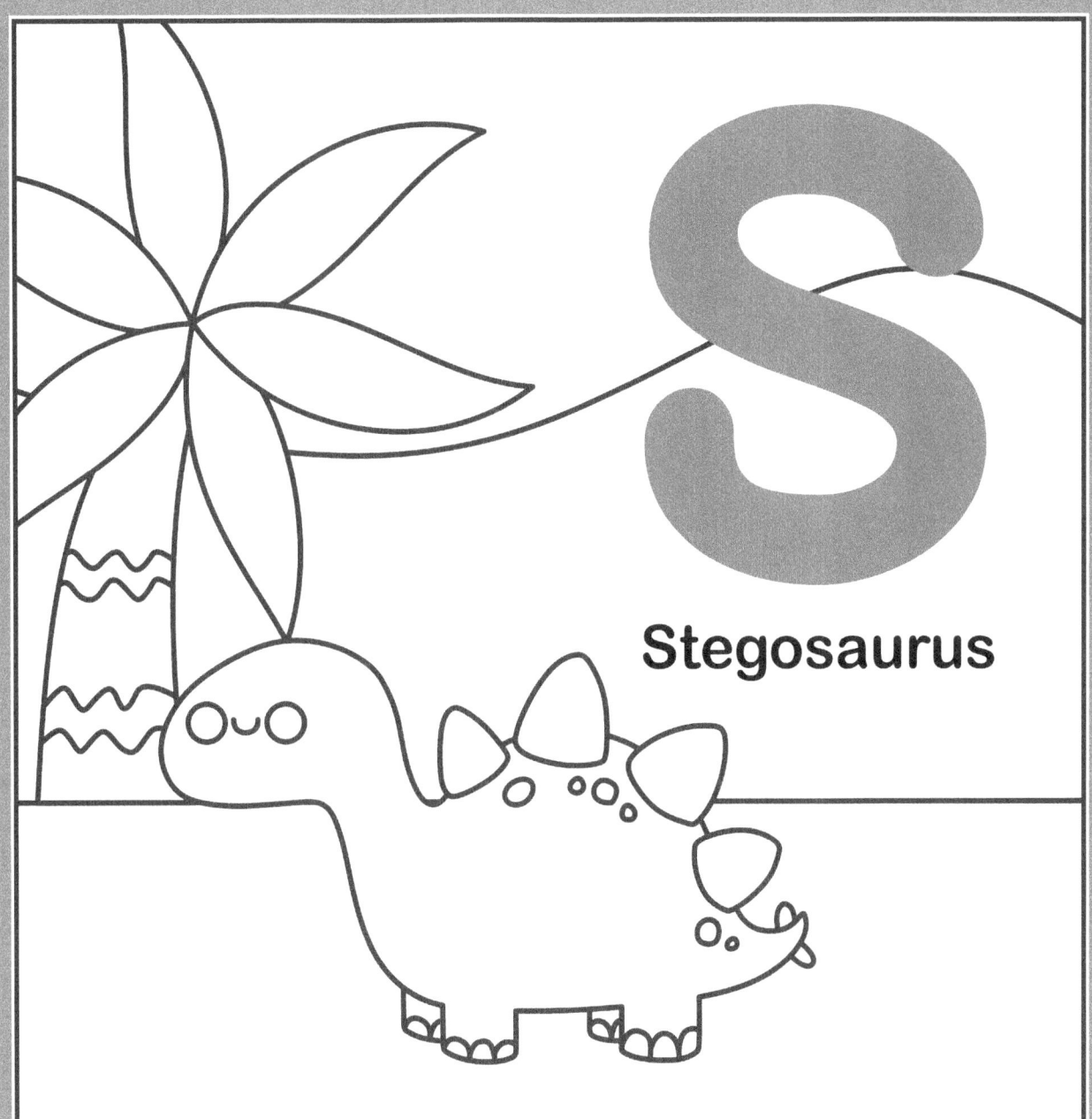

Stegosaurus

Write the letter:

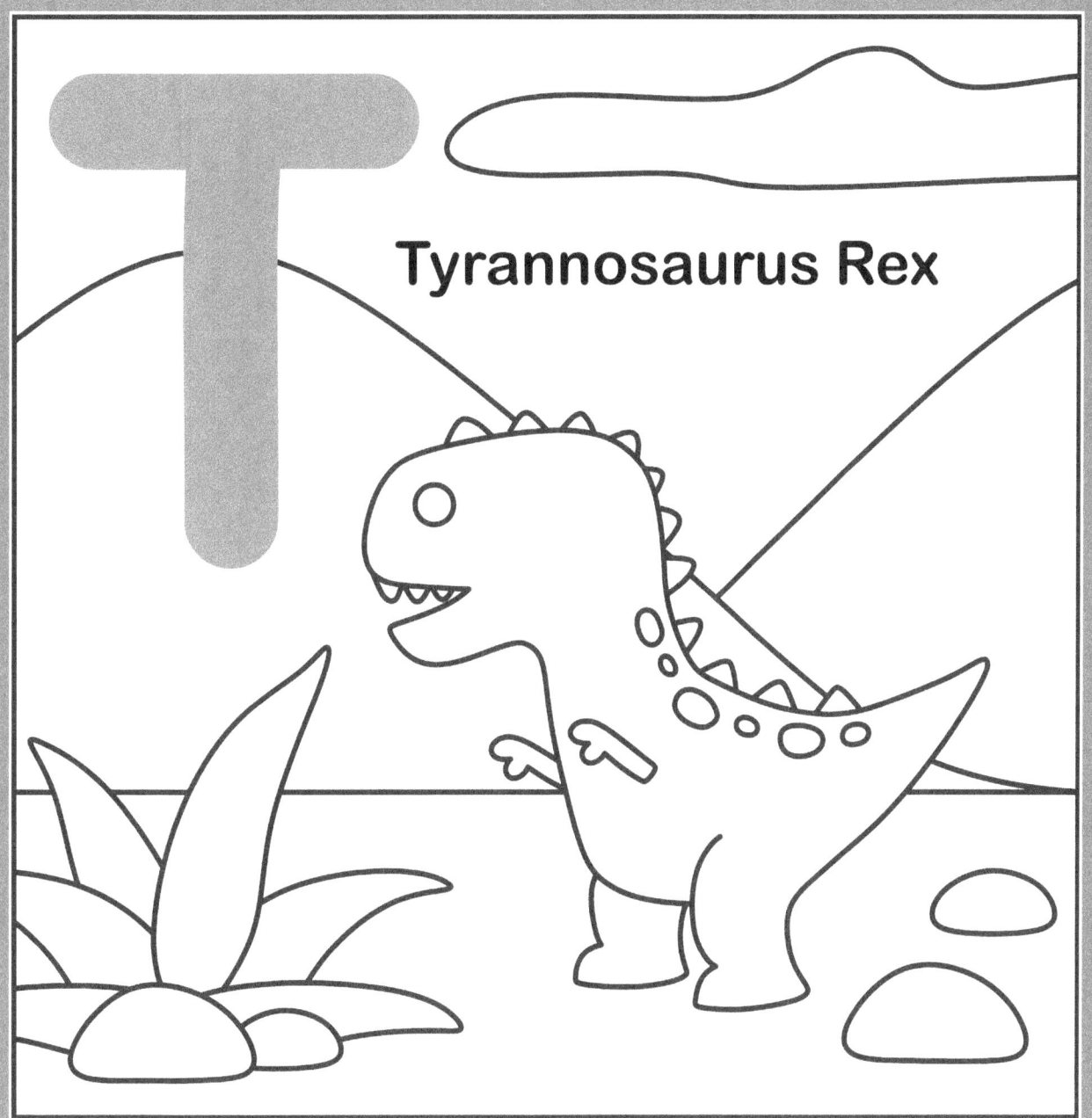

Tyrannosaurus Rex

Write the letter:

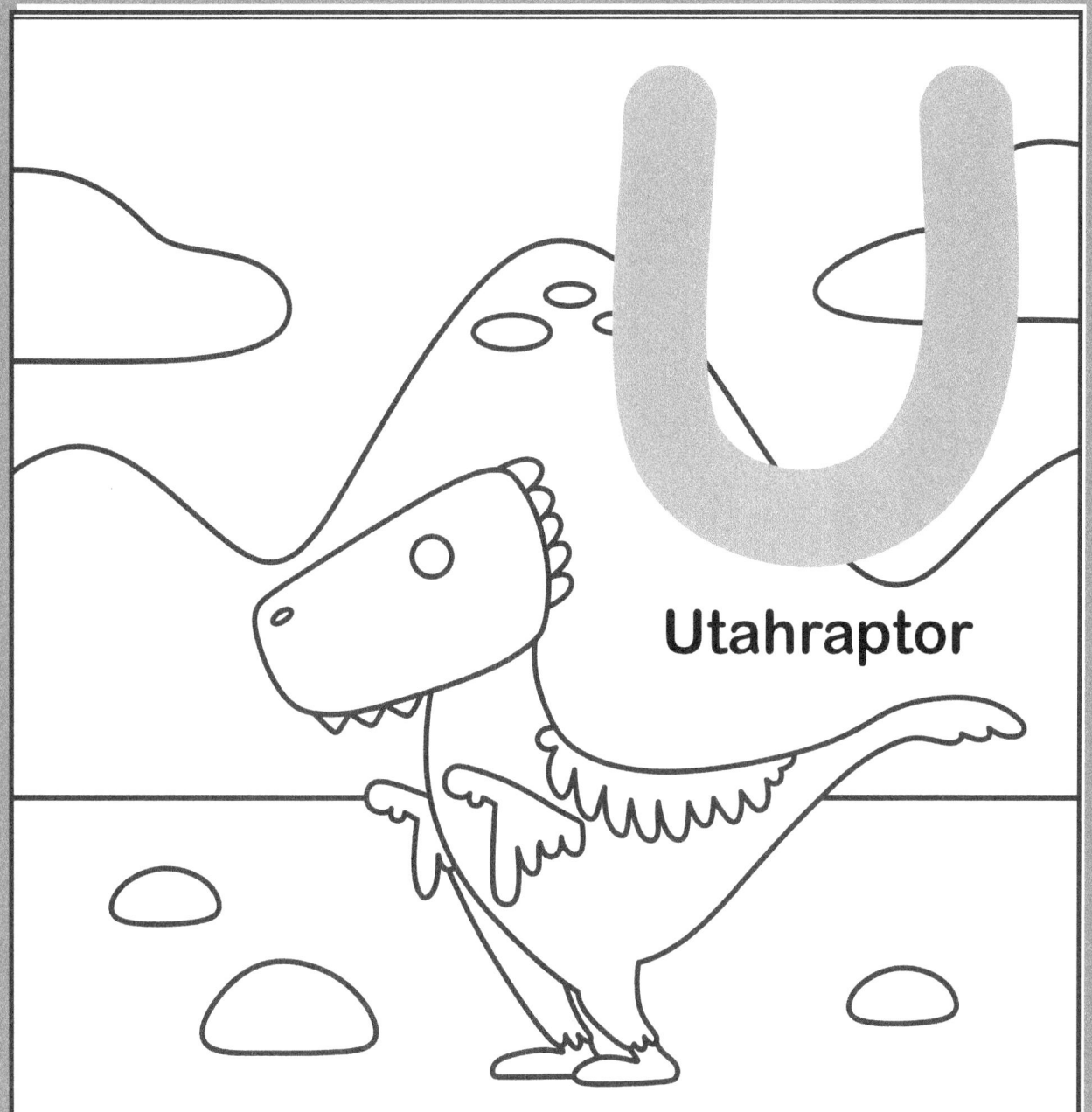

Utahraptor

Write the letter:

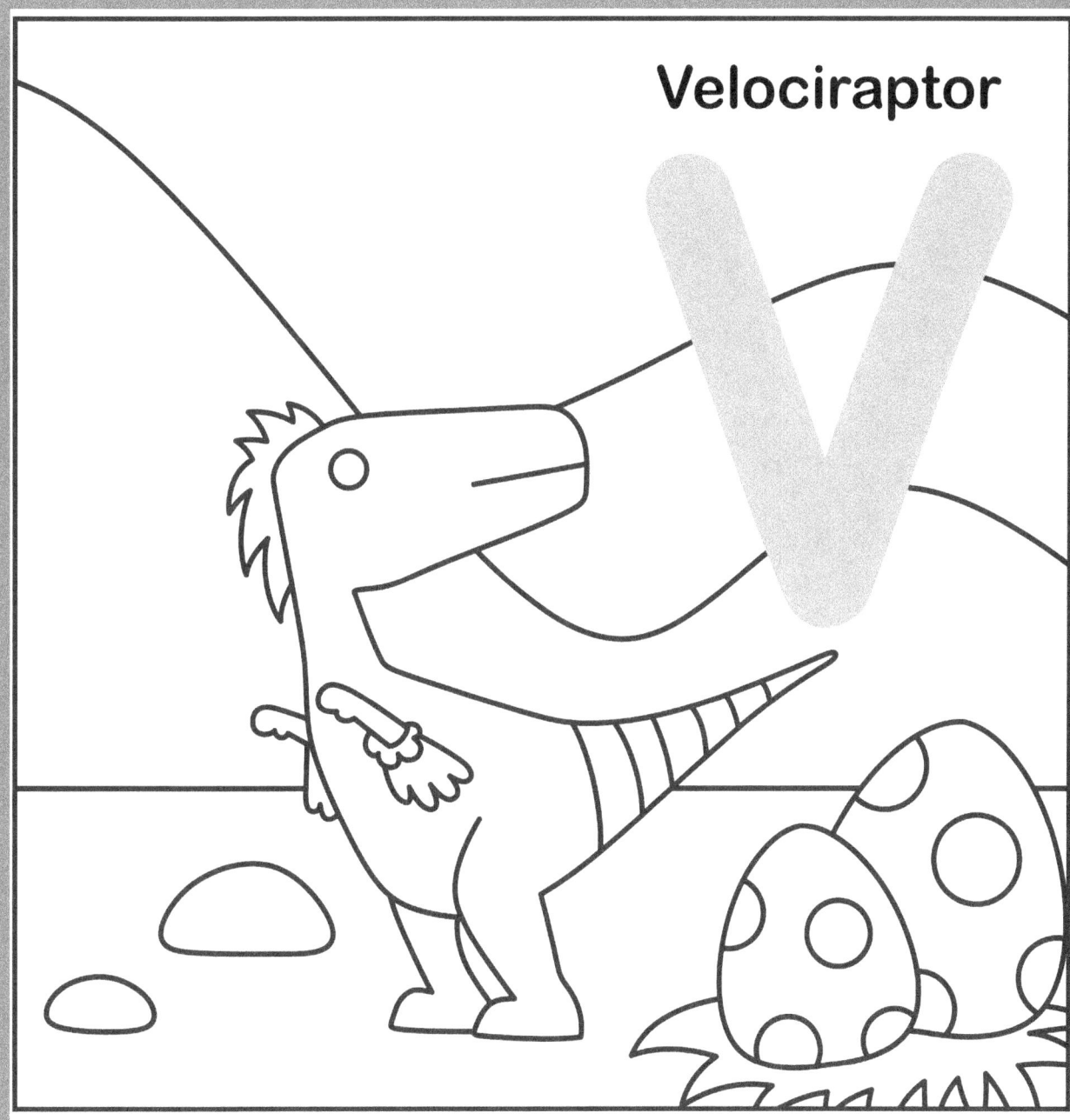

Velociraptor

Write the letter:

Wannosaurus

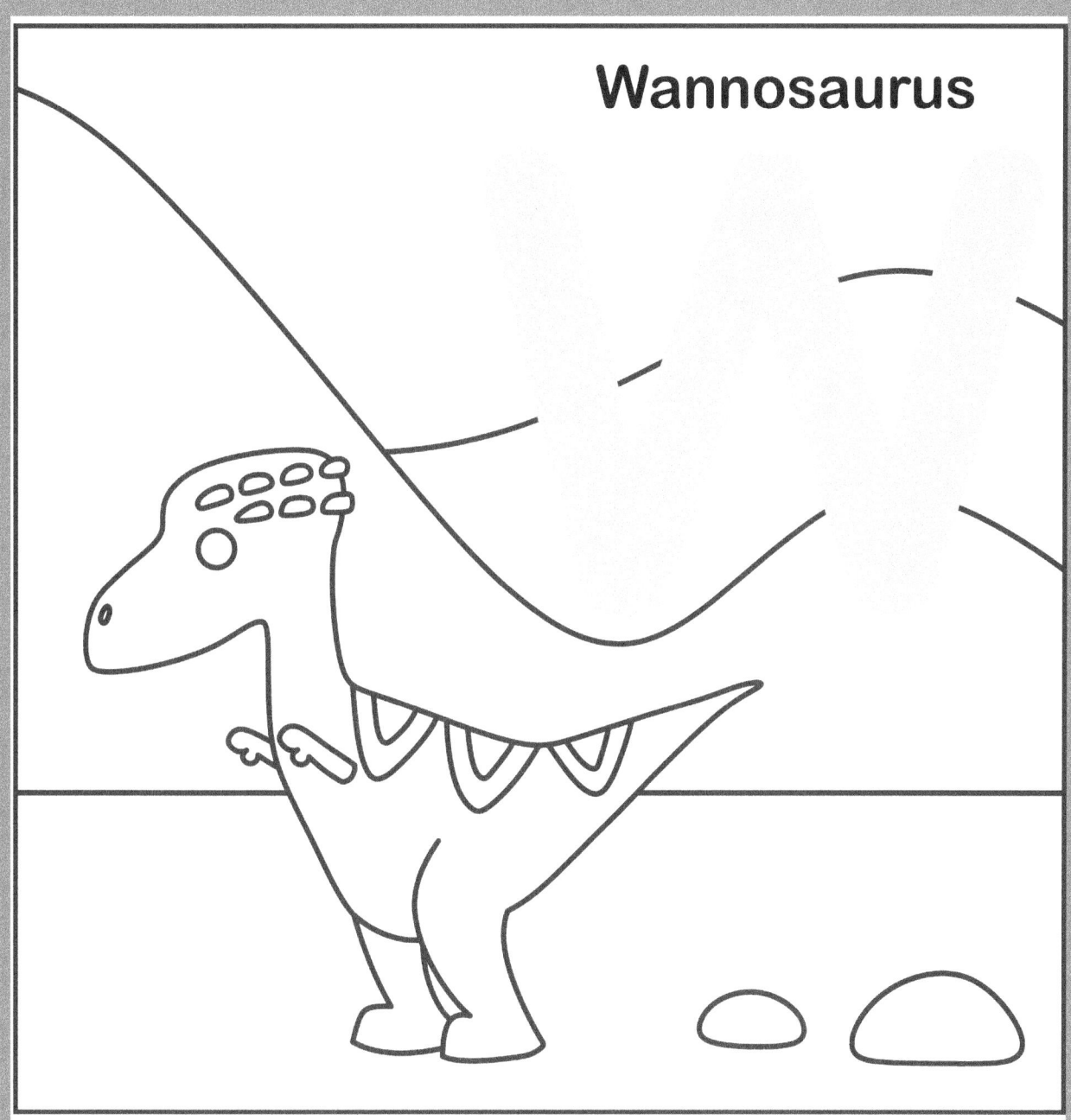

Write the letter:

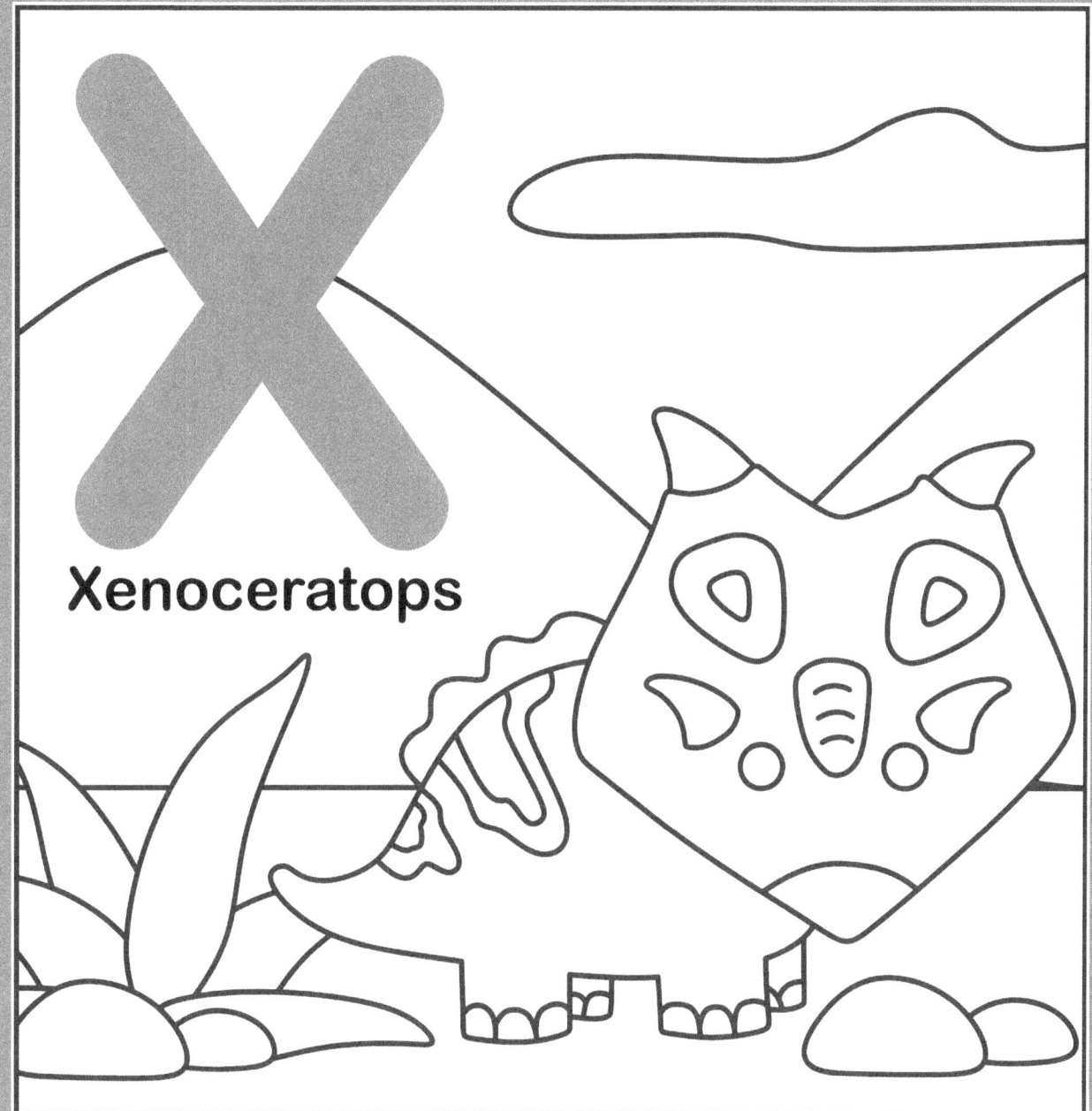

X
Xenoceratops

Write the letter:

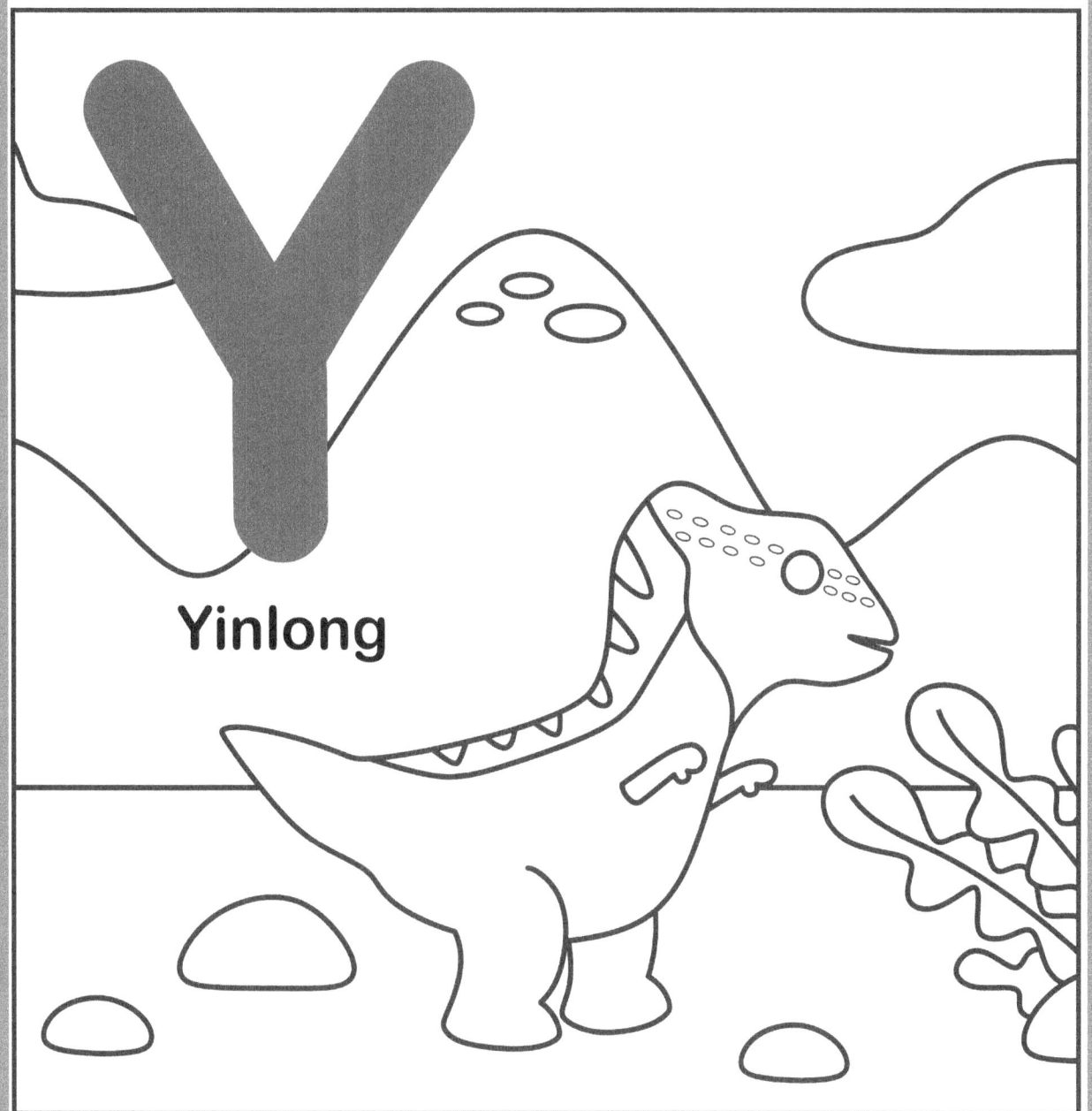

Yinlong

Write the letter:

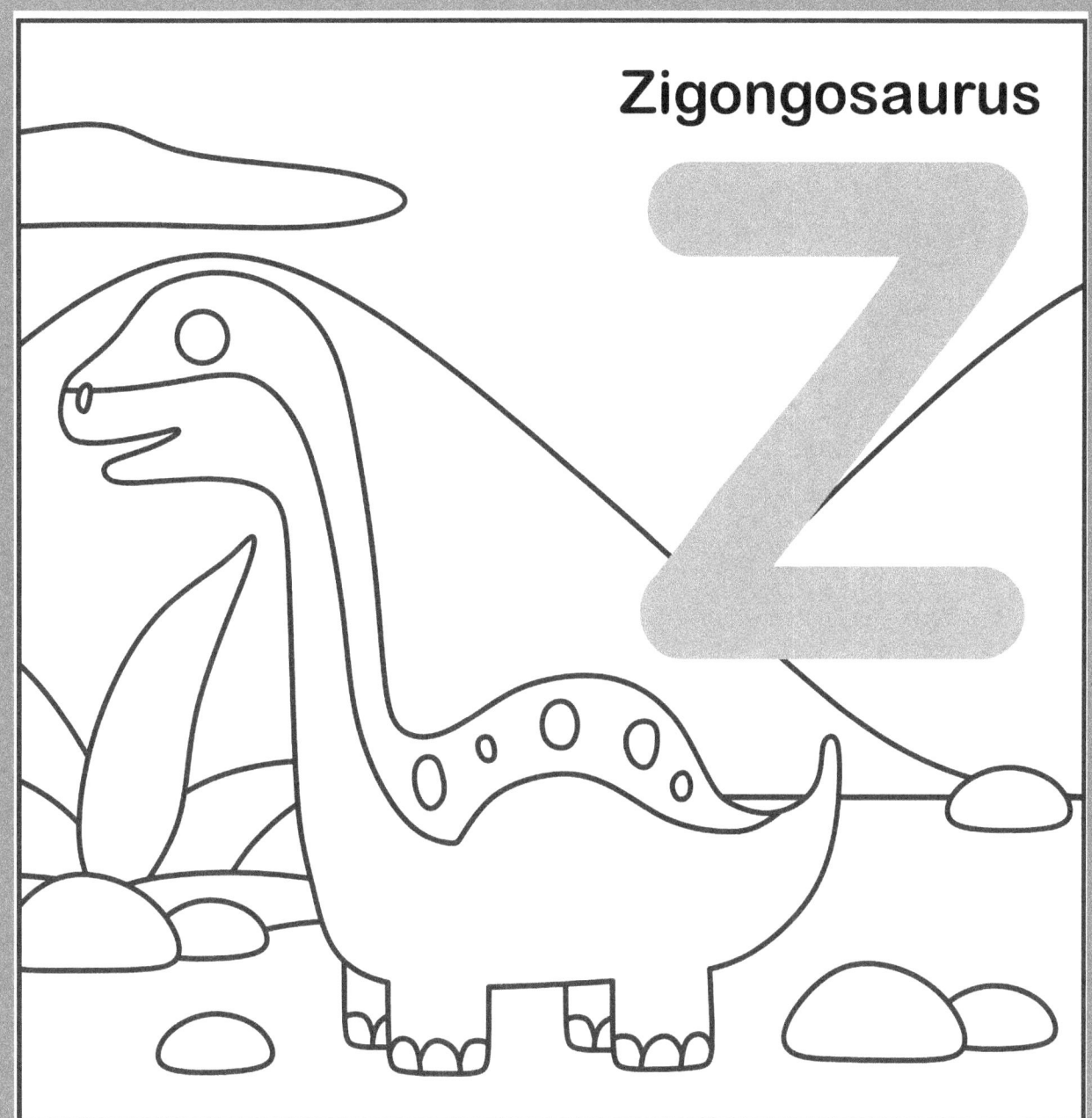

Zigongosaurus

Write the letter:

www.ingramcontent.com/pod-product-compliance
Lightning Source LLC
Chambersburg PA
CBHW060005230526
45472CB00008B/1956